# The Path to Spiritual Enlightenment: A Guide to Mindfulness and Meditation

Meditation can wipe away the day's stress, bringing with it inner peace.

# Table Of Contents

01

# Chapter 1: Introduction to Spiritual Enlightenment

# Understanding the Path to Enlightenment

Understanding the Path to Enlightenment is a crucial aspect of embarking on a journey towards spiritual growth and self-discovery. In the realm of spiritualism, enlightenment is often seen as the ultimate goal, a state of profound wisdom, clarity, and inner peace that transcends the limitations of the physical world.

To reach enlightenment, one must first understand the nature of their own mind and consciousness. This involves practicing mindfulness and meditation, which are powerful tools for cultivating self-awareness and inner peace. By learning to quiet the mind and connect with the present moment, individuals can begin to unravel the layers of conditioning and ego that prevent them from experiencing true enlightenment.

Energy healing and chakra balancing are also essential components of the path to enlightenment. By working with the body's energy centers, known as chakras, individuals can release blockages and restore balance to their physical, emotional, and spiritual well-being. This process allows for a deeper connection to the higher self and the divine energies that guide us on our spiritual journey.

Ancient mysticism and esoteric traditions provide valuable insights into the nature of enlightenment, drawing on the wisdom of ancient cultures and spiritual practices. Shamanism and indigenous spiritual practices offer unique perspectives on connecting with the natural world and the spirit realm, while yoga and holistic wellness provide practical tools for aligning mind, body, and spirit.

Astrology and divination, crystal healing and gemstone therapy, sacred geometry and metaphysical studies all play a role in deepening our understanding of the spiritual path and the interconnectedness of all things. Spiritual retreats and pilgrimages offer opportunities for reflection and renewal, while spirit communication and mediumship provide avenues for connecting with loved ones and spirit guides.

Ultimately, the path to enlightenment is a personal journey that requires dedication, patience, and an open heart. By exploring the various aspects of spirituality and embracing practices that resonate with our individual beliefs and values, we can move closer to experiencing the profound transformation that comes with true enlightenment.

# Benefits of Mindfulness and Meditation

In the subchapter titled "Benefits of Mindfulness and Meditation," we will explore the numerous advantages that these practices offer to individuals on the path to spiritual enlightenment. Mindfulness and meditation have long been revered in spiritual traditions around the world for their ability to cultivate inner peace, clarity, and connection to the divine.

One of the primary benefits of mindfulness and meditation is their ability to calm the mind and reduce stress. By focusing on the present moment and letting go of worries about the past or future, practitioners can experience a sense of relaxation and ease. This can have profound effects on both mental and physical health, as chronic stress has been linked to a variety of ailments.

Additionally, mindfulness and meditation can help individuals develop a deeper sense of self-awareness and self-compassion. By observing their thoughts and emotions without judgment, practitioners can gain insight into their inner workings and cultivate greater self-acceptance. This can lead to improved relationships, increased confidence, and a greater sense of fulfillment in life. Furthermore, mindfulness and meditation have been shown to enhance spiritual growth and connection to higher realms of consciousness. By quieting the mind and opening the heart, practitioners can experience profound states of peace, bliss, and unity with all beings. This can lead to a greater sense of purpose and alignment with one's true essence.

Overall, the benefits of mindfulness and meditation are vast and varied, making them essential tools for anyone seeking spiritual enlightenment. By incorporating these practices into your daily routine, you can experience greater peace, clarity, and connection to the divine within and around you.

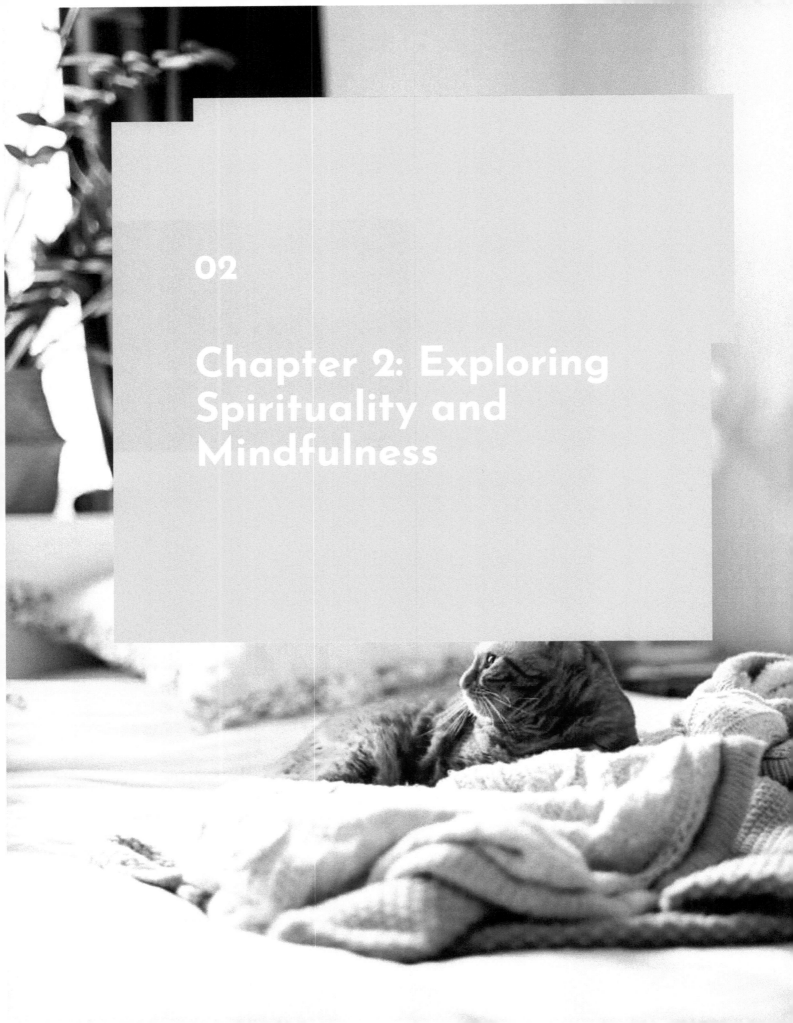

**02**

# Chapter 2: Exploring Spirituality and Mindfulness

# The Connection Between Spirituality and Mindfulness

In the subchapter "The Connection Between Spirituality and Mindfulness," we delve into the intrinsic relationship between these two practices and how they can work together to enhance our spiritual journey. Mindfulness, defined as the practice of being present in the moment with non-judgmental awareness, is a key component of many spiritual traditions. By cultivating mindfulness, we can deepen our connection to the divine and increase our spiritual awareness.

Spirituality, on the other hand, is the belief in something greater than ourselves and the quest for meaning and purpose in life. It is through spiritual practices such as meditation, prayer, and energy healing that we can nurture our spiritual growth and connect with the higher realms of existence. When we combine mindfulness with spirituality, we can access a deeper level of consciousness and tap into the universal energy that surrounds us.

By practicing mindfulness, we can quiet the chatter of our minds and create space for spiritual insights and revelations to come through. This heightened state of awareness allows us to tune into our intuition and receive guidance from our higher selves and spiritual guides. In this way, mindfulness becomes a powerful tool for enhancing our spiritual connection and deepening our understanding of the mysteries of the universe.

As we explore the connection between spirituality and mindfulness, we begin to see how these practices complement each other and lead us on a path to spiritual enlightenment. By incorporating mindfulness into our spiritual routines, we can cultivate a deeper sense of peace, clarity, and presence in our lives. This integration of mindfulness and spirituality opens the door to profound spiritual experiences and transformations that can help us align with our true purpose and highest potential.

## Techniques for Cultivating Mindfulness

In the subchapter "Techniques for Cultivating Mindfulness," we will explore various methods and practices that can help you deepen your sense of awareness and presence in the present moment. Mindfulness is the practice of paying attention to the present moment without judgment, allowing us to cultivate a sense of inner peace and clarity.

One technique for cultivating mindfulness is through meditation. By taking the time to sit quietly and focus on your breath, you can train your mind to be more present and attentive. There are many different types of meditation, such as mindfulness meditation, loving-kindness meditation, and body scan meditation, so you can choose the one that resonates most with you.

Another technique for cultivating mindfulness is through mindful movement practices, such as yoga or tai chi. These practices combine movement with breath awareness, helping you to stay grounded and focused in the present moment.

You can also cultivate mindfulness through daily activities, such as eating mindfully, walking in nature, or even washing the dishes with full awareness. By bringing a sense of mindfulness to these everyday tasks, you can train your mind to be more present and engaged in each moment.

In addition to these practices, you can also incorporate mindfulness into your daily routine by setting aside time for reflection, journaling, or gratitude practices. By taking the time to pause and reflect on your experiences, you can deepen your sense of mindfulness and connection to the present moment.

Overall, cultivating mindfulness is a journey that requires patience, practice, and dedication. By exploring these techniques and finding what works best for you, you can deepen your sense of awareness and presence in each moment, leading you on the path to spiritual enlightenment.

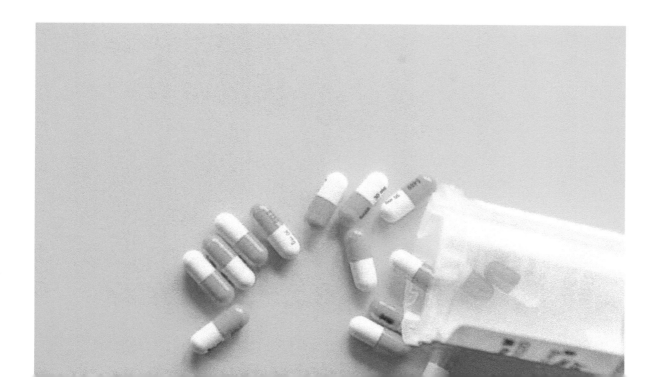

03

# Chapter 3: Energy Healing and Chakra Balancing

# Understanding Energy Healing

In the world of spirituality, energy healing is a practice that has been used for centuries to promote healing and balance in the mind, body, and spirit. This ancient practice is based on the belief that everything in the universe is made up of energy, and that this energy can be manipulated and directed to bring about healing and transformation.

Energy healing encompasses a wide range of practices, including Reiki, acupuncture, and crystal healing, all of which work to clear blockages in the body's energy centers, or chakras, and restore the natural flow of energy. By working with these energy centers, practitioners can help to release negative emotions, heal physical ailments, and promote overall well-being.

One of the key principles of energy healing is the idea that the body has an innate ability to heal itself, and that by tapping into this natural healing energy, individuals can support their own healing process. By working with a skilled energy healer, individuals can learn to harness their own energy and use it to promote healing and balance in their lives.

Energy healing is not just a physical practice; it also involves working with the mind and spirit to promote holistic healing and well-being. By combining energy healing with practices such as mindfulness, meditation, and yoga, individuals can create a powerful tool for personal transformation and spiritual growth.

Whether you are new to the world of energy healing or have been practicing for years, understanding the principles behind this ancient practice can help you to deepen your connection to yourself and the world around you. By exploring the world of energy healing, you can tap into a powerful source of healing and transformation that can help you to live a more balanced and fulfilling life.

## Balancing the Chakras for Spiritual Well-being

Balancing the chakras is essential for achieving spiritual well-being and inner harmony. The chakras are energy centers located along the spine, each corresponding to different aspects of our physical, emotional, and spiritual well-being. When these energy centers are blocked or unbalanced, it can lead to feelings of disconnection, emotional turmoil, and physical ailments.

In order to balance the chakras, it is important to first understand each one and its corresponding qualities. The root chakra, located at the base of the spine, is associated with grounding and survival instincts. The sacral chakra, located in the lower abdomen, is linked to creativity and emotional expression. The solar plexus chakra, located in the upper abdomen, governs personal power and self-esteem. The heart chakra, located in the center of the chest, is the center of love and compassion. The throat chakra, located in the throat, is connected to communication and self-expression. The third eye chakra, located between the eyebrows, is the center of intuition and inner wisdom. Finally, the crown chakra, located at the top of the head, is the connection to the divine and spiritual enlightenment.

Balancing the chakras can be achieved through various practices such as meditation, yoga, energy healing, and crystal therapy. By focusing on each chakra individually and using specific techniques to cleanse and align them, one can restore balance and harmony to their energy system. This can result in increased vitality, emotional stability, and a deeper connection to the spiritual realm.

Incorporating chakra balancing into your daily spiritual practice can have profound effects on your overall well-being. By aligning your energy centers and clearing any blockages, you can experience a greater sense of peace, clarity, and spiritual enlightenment. Take the time to explore the ancient wisdom of the chakras and discover the transformative power they hold for your spiritual journey.

04

# Chapter 4: Ancient Mysticism and Esoteric Traditions

# Exploring Ancient Spiritual Practices

In the subchapter "Exploring Ancient Spiritual Practices," we delve into the rich tapestry of wisdom passed down through the ages by our ancestors. These ancient spiritual practices provide us with a roadmap to connect with our higher selves, the universe, and the divine.

One of the most powerful tools in our spiritual arsenal is mindfulness and meditation. By quieting the mind and turning our attention inward, we gain access to a deeper level of awareness and understanding. Through these practices, we can cultivate a sense of peace, clarity, and presence that permeates every aspect of our lives.

Energy healing and chakra balancing are also vital components of ancient spiritual practices. By working with the subtle energies that flow through our bodies, we can align our chakras and remove blockages that may be holding us back. This allows for a greater flow of energy and vitality, promoting health and well-being on all levels.

Ancient mysticism and esoteric traditions offer us a glimpse into the hidden realms of existence. By exploring these teachings, we can expand our consciousness and tap into the universal truths that have been passed down through generations.

Shamanism and indigenous spiritual practices provide us with a deep connection to the earth and all living beings. By honoring the wisdom of our ancestors and the natural world, we can gain insight into our true purpose and place in the cosmos.

Yoga and holistic wellness practices offer us a way to integrate mind, body, and spirit. Through asana, pranayama, and meditation, we can cultivate a sense of balance and harmony that extends beyond the physical realm.

Astrology and divination provide us with a roadmap for understanding the cycles of the cosmos and how they impact our lives. By consulting the stars and the cards, we can gain insight into our past, present, and future, guiding us on our spiritual journey.

Crystal healing and gemstone therapy harness the power of the earth's energies to promote healing and transformation. By working with these sacred tools, we can align our vibrations with the frequencies of the universe, bringing about profound shifts in our consciousness.

Sacred geometry and metaphysical studies offer us a window into the underlying patterns of creation. By exploring the mathematical and geometric principles that underpin the universe, we can gain a deeper understanding of the interconnectedness of all things. Spiritual retreats and pilgrimages provide us with an opportunity to step out of our daily lives and immerse ourselves in the sacred. By journeying to sacred sites and engaging in spiritual practices with like-minded individuals, we can deepen our connection to the divine and experience profound spiritual transformation.

Spirit communication and mediumship offer us a way to connect with the spirit world and receive guidance from our ancestors and guides. By developing our intuitive abilities and opening ourselves up to the messages of the unseen realms, we can gain insight and wisdom that can help us navigate our spiritual path.

In conclusion, exploring ancient spiritual practices offers us a pathway to connect with the timeless wisdom of our ancestors and the universal truths that transcend time and space. By incorporating these practices into our daily lives, we can cultivate a deeper sense of connection, purpose, and fulfillment on our journey to spiritual enlightenment.

## Incorporating Esoteric Traditions into Modern Life

As we continue on our journey of spiritual enlightenment, it is important to recognize the value of incorporating esoteric traditions into our modern lives. These ancient practices and beliefs hold a wealth of wisdom and insight that can help us deepen our understanding of ourselves and the world around us.

One way to incorporate esoteric traditions into modern life is through mindfulness and meditation. By tapping into the wisdom of ancient mysticism and esoteric traditions, we can enhance our meditation practice and cultivate a sense of inner peace and clarity. Practices such as energy healing and chakra balancing can also help us align our energy centers and promote overall well-being.

Shamanism and indigenous spiritual practices offer another avenue for incorporating esoteric traditions into modern life. By connecting with the natural world and honoring the wisdom of our ancestors, we can gain a deeper sense of connection and purpose. Yoga and holistic wellness practices can also help us integrate esoteric teachings into our daily routine, promoting balance and harmony in mind, body, and spirit.

For those interested in exploring divination and astrology, incorporating esoteric traditions into modern life can provide valuable insights and guidance. By working with crystals, gemstones, and sacred geometry, we can tap into the healing properties of these ancient tools and enhance our spiritual practice.

Whether through spiritual retreats, pilgrimages, or spirit communication and mediumship, there are countless ways to incorporate esoteric traditions into modern life. By embracing these ancient practices and beliefs, we can deepen our spiritual connection and bring a sense of magic and wonder into our everyday experiences.

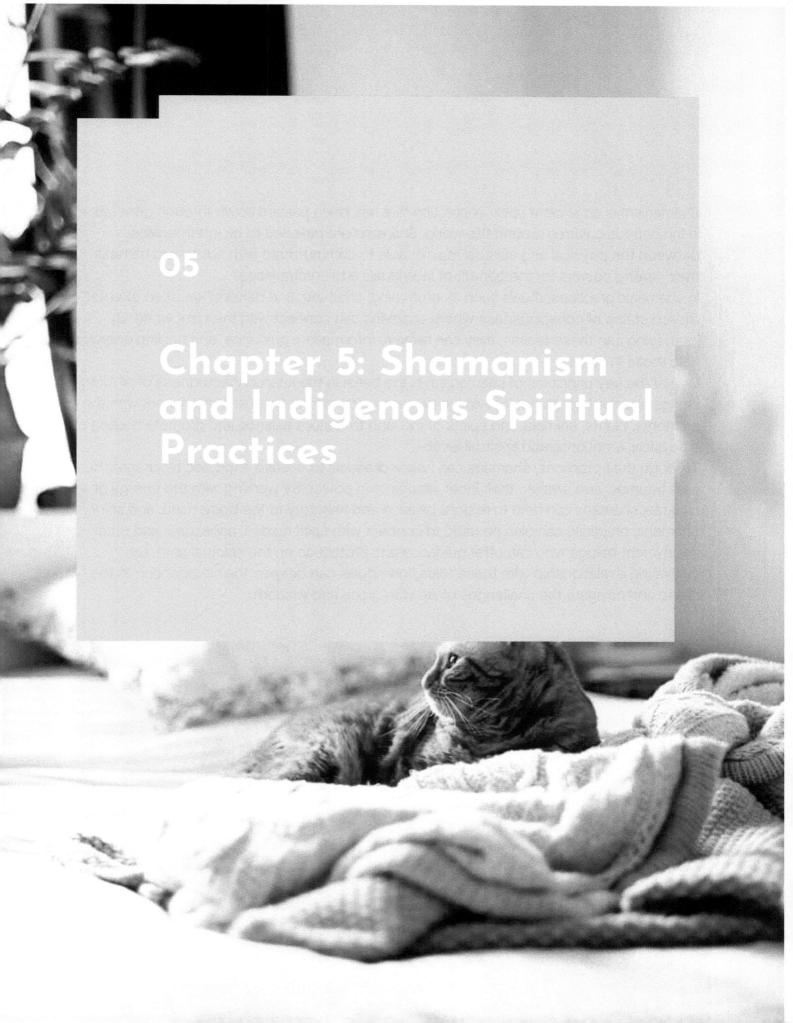

05

# Chapter 5: Shamanism and Indigenous Spiritual Practices

# Understanding Shamanic Practices

Shamanism is an ancient spiritual practice that has been passed down through generations in indigenous cultures around the world. Shamans are believed to be intermediaries between the physical and spiritual realms, able to communicate with spirits and harness their healing powers for the benefit of individuals and communities.

In shamanic practices, rituals such as drumming, chanting, and dancing are used to enter altered states of consciousness where shamans can connect with the spirit world. By journeying into these realms, they can retrieve information, guidance, and healing energy to help those in need.

One of the key principles of shamanism is the belief in the interconnectedness of all living beings and the importance of living in harmony with nature. Shamans often work with the elements, plants, animals, and spirits of the land to restore balance and promote healing on a physical, emotional, and spiritual level.

Through their practices, shamans can help individuals to release energetic blockages, heal past traumas, and awaken their inner wisdom and power. By working with the energy of the chakras, shamans can help to restore balance and harmony to the body, mind, and spirit.

Shamanic practices can also be used to connect with spirit guides, ancestors, and other benevolent beings who can offer guidance and protection on the spiritual path. By cultivating a relationship with these allies, individuals can deepen their connection to the divine and navigate the challenges of life with grace and wisdom.

Overall, understanding shamanic practices can offer valuable insights and tools for spiritual growth, healing, and transformation. By embracing the wisdom of the shamans, we can tap into the universal energies that surround us and awaken to our true potential as spiritual beings on a journey of enlightenment.

# Connecting with Indigenous Spiritual Wisdom

In the subchapter "Connecting with Indigenous Spiritual Wisdom," we delve into the profound teachings and practices of indigenous cultures around the world. These ancient traditions hold a wealth of knowledge and wisdom that can greatly enhance our spiritual journey and deepen our connection to the Earth and the cosmos.

Indigenous spiritual wisdom emphasizes the interconnectedness of all beings and the importance of living in harmony with nature. By learning from these traditions, we can gain a greater appreciation for the natural world and our place within it. Practices such as honoring the elements, working with plant medicine, and connecting with spirit guides can help us tap into a deeper sense of purpose and belonging.

Shamanism, a central aspect of many indigenous cultures, offers powerful tools for healing and transformation. Through practices such as journeying, soul retrieval, and energy clearing, we can address deep-seated wounds and blockages that may be holding us back on our spiritual path. By embracing the wisdom of the shamanic tradition, we can access higher states of consciousness and cultivate a deeper connection to the spiritual realms.

Incorporating indigenous spiritual practices into our mindfulness and meditation routine can help us expand our awareness and open ourselves up to new possibilities. By honoring the wisdom of our ancestors and indigenous elders, we can cultivate a sense of gratitude and reverence for the gifts of the Earth and the wisdom of the cosmos. Whether through participating in sacred ceremonies, working with indigenous healers, or simply spending time in nature, connecting with indigenous spiritual wisdom can be a transformative and enriching experience for those on the path to spiritual enlightenment. It is a reminder of the interconnectedness of all things and the importance of living in harmony with the Earth and all beings.

# Chapter 6: Yoga and Holistic Wellness

# The Spiritual Benefits of Yoga

In the subchapter "The Spiritual Benefits of Yoga," we delve into the profound impact that the ancient practice of yoga can have on our spiritual journey. Yoga is not just a physical exercise; it is a holistic approach to uniting the body, mind, and spirit. Through the practice of yoga, we can tap into our innermost being and connect with the divine energy that flows through all of creation.

One of the key spiritual benefits of yoga is the deep sense of inner peace and tranquility that it can bring. By focusing on the breath and moving through the poses, we can quiet the chatter of the mind and enter a state of deep meditation. In this stillness, we can hear the whispers of our soul and connect with our higher self.

Yoga also helps to balance and align the chakras, the energy centers within the body. By practicing specific poses and breathing techniques, we can clear blockages in our energy field and restore harmony to our physical, emotional, and spiritual bodies. This can lead to a greater sense of vitality and well-being, as well as a heightened awareness of our spiritual nature.

Furthermore, yoga can help us to cultivate mindfulness and presence in our daily lives. By bringing our awareness to the present moment, we can let go of worries about the past and future and simply be here now. This can help us to experience life more fully and connect with the divine essence that is always present within us.

Overall, the spiritual benefits of yoga are vast and profound. By incorporating this ancient practice into our spiritual journey, we can deepen our connection to the divine, awaken our inner wisdom, and experience true spiritual enlightenment.

# Holistic Approaches to Wellness

In the quest for spiritual enlightenment, it is crucial to adopt holistic approaches to wellness that encompass all aspects of our being - mind, body, and soul. By taking a holistic approach, we can achieve a deeper level of balance and harmony within ourselves, leading to a greater sense of spiritual fulfillment. One of the key pillars of holistic wellness is mindfulness and meditation. These practices help us to quiet the mind, focus on the present moment, and connect with our inner selves. By incorporating mindfulness and meditation into our daily routine, we can cultivate a sense of peace and clarity that will aid us on our spiritual journey.

Energy healing and chakra balancing are also essential components of holistic wellness. By working to balance the energy centers within our bodies, known as chakras, we can remove blockages and promote the free flow of life force energy. This can lead to improved physical, emotional, and spiritual well-being.

Ancient mysticism and esoteric traditions offer valuable insights and practices for those seeking spiritual enlightenment. By delving into the wisdom of ancient cultures and traditions, we can gain a deeper understanding of the interconnectedness of all things and our place in the universe.

Shamanism and indigenous spiritual practices provide powerful tools for healing and transformation. By connecting with the natural world and honoring the wisdom of our ancestors, we can tap into a source of wisdom and guidance that transcends the limitations of our everyday lives.

Yoga and holistic wellness practices offer a comprehensive approach to healing and spiritual growth. By incorporating practices such as yoga, meditation, breathwork, and bodywork into our daily routine, we can cultivate a sense of balance and well-being that extends to all areas of our lives.

Astrology and divination can also provide valuable insights into our spiritual path. By exploring the movements of the planets and stars, we can gain a deeper understanding of the forces at play in our lives and how we can align ourselves with the cosmic energies for greater spiritual growth.

Crystal healing and gemstone therapy offer powerful tools for energetic healing and transformation. By working with the healing properties of crystals and gemstones, we can clear negative energy, balance our chakras, and enhance our spiritual connection.

Sacred geometry and metaphysical studies provide a framework for understanding the underlying patterns and structures of the universe. By exploring sacred geometry and metaphysical principles, we can gain insights into the interconnectedness of all things and the underlying unity of creation.

Spiritual retreats and pilgrimages offer opportunities for deepening our spiritual practice and connecting with like-minded individuals. By immersing ourselves in sacred spaces and engaging in spiritual practices with others, we can accelerate our spiritual growth and deepen our connection to the divine.

Finally, spirit communication and mediumship can provide a bridge to the spiritual realms and offer guidance and wisdom from the higher planes. By developing our abilities to communicate with spirits and receive messages from the other side, we can gain valuable insights and guidance for our spiritual journey.

In conclusion, by embracing holistic approaches to wellness that encompass mindfulness, energy healing, ancient wisdom, shamanism, yoga, astrology, crystal healing, sacred geometry, spiritual retreats, and spirit communication, we can accelerate our spiritual growth and deepen our connection to the divine. By incorporating these practices into our daily lives, we can cultivate a sense of balance, harmony, and peace that will guide us on the path to spiritual enlightenment.

07

# Chapter 7: Astrology and Divination

# Exploring Astrology and Its Role in Spiritual Growth

Astrology has been a tool for spiritual growth and self-discovery for centuries. By exploring the movements of the planets and the alignment of the stars, individuals can gain insight into their own personalities, strengths, and weaknesses. Astrology can help us understand our purpose in life, our relationships with others, and the challenges we may face on our spiritual journey.

In astrology, each person is believed to be influenced by the unique energy of the planets at the time of their birth. By studying our birth chart, we can uncover hidden talents, desires, and obstacles that may be holding us back from reaching our full potential. Astrology can also provide guidance on how to navigate difficult times and make important decisions in alignment with our true selves.

For those on a path to spiritual enlightenment, astrology can be a valuable tool for self-reflection and growth. By understanding the energies at play in our lives, we can learn to work with them rather than against them. Astrology can help us recognize patterns and cycles in our behavior, allowing us to make positive changes and break free from negative habits.

By incorporating astrology into our spiritual practice, we can deepen our connection to the universe and gain a greater understanding of our place within it. Whether we are seeking guidance on love, career, or personal development, astrology can offer valuable insights and support on our journey towards enlightenment. Through the study of astrology, we can unlock the mysteries of the cosmos and discover our true purpose in life.

# Using Divination Tools for Spiritual Guidance

Divination tools have been used for centuries by spiritual seekers seeking guidance, clarity, and insight into the mysteries of life. From ancient civilizations to modern practitioners, these tools have been seen as powerful aids in connecting with the spiritual realm and receiving messages from higher sources.

One of the most popular divination tools is the Tarot deck, a set of cards with symbolic imagery that can be used to tap into the subconscious mind and receive guidance on various aspects of life. Each card in the deck carries its own unique energy and message, which can be interpreted by the reader to gain deeper insights into their current situation or future path.

Another widely used divination tool is the pendulum, a weighted object suspended on a chain or cord that can be used to answer yes or no questions or to uncover hidden truths. By tuning into the subtle movements of the pendulum, practitioners can access their intuition and receive guidance from the spiritual realm.

Other divination tools include runes, crystals, astrology charts, and more, each offering their own unique method of tapping into the unseen forces of the universe. Whether you are seeking guidance on love, career, health, or any other aspect of life, divination tools can provide you with the clarity and insight you need to make informed decisions and navigate your spiritual journey with confidence.

By incorporating divination tools into your spiritual practice, you can deepen your connection to the spiritual realm, access higher wisdom, and receive the guidance and support you need to navigate life's challenges and opportunities. Trust in the power of these tools and allow them to guide you on your path to spiritual enlightenment.

# Chapter 8: Crystal Healing and Gemstone Therapy

# Harnessing the Power of Crystals for Healing

In the realm of spirituality and energy healing, harnessing the power of crystals for healing is a practice that has been utilized for centuries. Crystals are believed to hold unique energetic properties that can help balance the body, mind, and spirit. By incorporating crystals into your mindfulness and meditation practices, you can enhance your spiritual journey and promote overall well-being.

Crystals are often used in energy healing and chakra balancing to help clear blockages and restore harmony to the body's energy centers. Each crystal is said to resonate with a specific chakra, making it a powerful tool for healing and alignment. For example, amethyst is associated with the crown chakra and is believed to promote spiritual growth and connection, while rose quartz is linked to the heart chakra and is said to encourage love and compassion.

In addition to chakra balancing, crystals can also be used for protection, manifestation, and intention setting. By setting intentions and working with specific crystals, you can amplify your manifestations and bring your desires into reality. Whether you seek abundance, love, or healing, there is a crystal to support your intentions and goals.

To incorporate crystals into your spiritual practice, start by selecting crystals that resonate with you and your intentions. Cleanse and charge your crystals regularly to maintain their energetic properties and keep them aligned with your goals. You can place crystals on your body during meditation, create crystal grids, or simply carry them with you throughout the day to benefit from their healing energies.

By harnessing the power of crystals for healing, you can deepen your spiritual practice, enhance your mindfulness and meditation experiences, and align with the universal energies that support your spiritual journey. Explore the world of crystal healing and discover the transformative power of these ancient and sacred tools.

# Gemstone Therapy for Spiritual Alignment

Gemstone therapy is a powerful tool for aligning your spiritual energy and achieving a deeper connection with your inner self. Each gemstone is believed to carry its own unique vibration and healing properties, making them ideal for balancing the chakras and promoting spiritual growth.

In the practice of gemstone therapy, different stones are used to address specific spiritual concerns. For example, amethyst is often used to enhance intuition and spiritual awareness, while rose quartz is known for promoting love and compassion. By incorporating these gemstones into your meditation and mindfulness practices, you can enhance the energy flow throughout your body and achieve a greater sense of spiritual alignment.

One way to incorporate gemstone therapy into your spiritual practice is by creating a gemstone grid. This involves arranging various gemstones in a pattern that corresponds to the energy centers of the body, known as the chakras. By meditating with this grid, you can focus on balancing and aligning your spiritual energy, allowing for a deeper sense of connection with the divine.

Another technique for using gemstones for spiritual alignment is to wear them as jewelry or carry them with you throughout the day. This allows you to benefit from the healing properties of the stones continuously, promoting a sense of peace and harmony in your daily life.

Overall, gemstone therapy can be a valuable tool for anyone seeking spiritual enlightenment and alignment. By incorporating the energy of these powerful stones into your spiritual practice, you can enhance your connection to the divine and experience a greater sense of inner peace and clarity.

09

# Chapter 9: Sacred Geometry and Metaphysical Studies

# Exploring the Sacred Geometry of the Universe

In the subchapter "Exploring the Sacred Geometry of the Universe," we delve into the ancient wisdom that teaches us about the interconnectedness of all things through geometric patterns and symbols. Sacred geometry is a powerful tool for spiritual growth and enlightenment, as it helps us connect with the divine energy that flows through the universe.

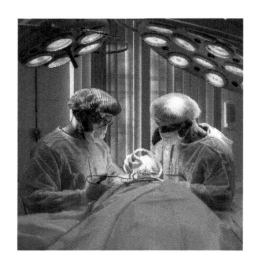

Through the study of sacred geometry, we can unlock the secrets of the universe and gain a deeper understanding of our place within it. The shapes and patterns found in sacred geometry, such as the flower of life, the golden ratio, and the Fibonacci sequence, all hold profound significance and meaning that can guide us on our spiritual journey.

By meditating on these geometric symbols, we can align ourselves with the harmonious energy of the cosmos and tap into the universal consciousness that surrounds us. This practice can help us achieve a sense of peace, balance, and clarity in our lives, allowing us to connect with our higher selves and the divine source of all creation.

Whether you are drawn to the intricate patterns of the mandala, the symmetry of the Sri Yantra, or the simplicity of the circle, exploring the sacred geometry of the universe can be a transformative experience that deepens your spiritual connection and enhances your mindfulness and meditation practices.

As we open ourselves up to the wisdom of sacred geometry, we may begin to see the world in a new light – as a vast tapestry of interconnected energies and vibrations that shape our reality. Through this exploration, we can unlock the secrets of the universe and discover the true nature of our spiritual essence.

# Metaphysical Studies for Spiritual Enlightenment

In the journey towards spiritual enlightenment, the exploration of metaphysical studies plays a crucial role in expanding our understanding of the universe and our place within it. By delving into the realms beyond the physical, we can tap into a deeper level of consciousness and connect with the spiritual energies that surround us. One of the key aspects of metaphysical studies is the exploration of sacred geometry, which reveals the underlying patterns and structures that govern the natural world. By studying geometric shapes such as the Flower of Life or the Sri Yantra, we can gain insights into the interconnectedness of all things and the divine order that permeates the universe.

Another important aspect of metaphysical studies is the practice of energy healing and chakra balancing. By working with the subtle energies that flow through our bodies, we can release blockages and restore harmony to our physical, emotional, and spiritual well-being. Through practices such as Reiki, Qi Gong, and crystal healing, we can cleanse and activate our chakras, bringing them into alignment and allowing for the free flow of energy throughout our being.

Metaphysical studies also encompass the exploration of ancient mysticism and esoteric traditions, such as alchemy, Kabbalah, and Hermeticism. By delving into these ancient teachings, we can uncover hidden wisdom and unlock the secrets of the universe. These teachings offer profound insights into the nature of reality and the interconnectedness of all things, guiding us towards a deeper understanding of our true selves and our purpose in this world.

Incorporating metaphysical studies into our spiritual practice can lead to profound transformation and enlightenment. By opening ourselves up to the mysteries of the universe and embracing the spiritual energies that surround us, we can deepen our connection to the divine and awaken to our true potential as spiritual beings. Through the exploration of sacred geometry, energy healing, and ancient mysticism, we can expand our consciousness and embark on a journey towards spiritual enlightenment.

# 10

# Chapter 10: Spiritual Retreats and Pilgrimages

# The Importance of Spiritual Retreats

In the journey towards spiritual enlightenment, one powerful tool that can greatly aid in personal growth and self-discovery is the practice of spiritual retreats. These retreats provide a sacred space away from the distractions of everyday life, allowing individuals to deepen their connection to their inner selves and the divine.

One of the key benefits of spiritual retreats is the opportunity for introspection and reflection. By taking time away from the hustle and bustle of daily life, individuals can quiet the mind and listen to the whispers of their soul. This introspective process can lead to profound insights and a deeper understanding of one's true purpose and path in life.

Spiritual retreats also provide a supportive and nurturing environment for personal growth and healing. Whether through mindfulness practices, meditation, energy healing, or other spiritual modalities, participants can release emotional baggage, heal past wounds, and cultivate a sense of inner peace and balance.

Moreover, spiritual retreats often offer the chance to connect with like-minded individuals on a similar spiritual journey. This sense of community and shared experience can be incredibly empowering and uplifting, providing a sense of belonging and support that is invaluable on the path to spiritual enlightenment.

Whether you are drawn to ancient mysticism, shamanism, yoga, astrology, crystal healing, or any other spiritual tradition, there is a retreat out there that can cater to your unique interests and needs. By immersing yourself in the transformative energy of a spiritual retreat, you can accelerate your spiritual growth, deepen your connection to the divine, and experience profound shifts in consciousness that will stay with you long after the retreat has ended.

# Embarking on Pilgrimages for Spiritual Growth

Pilgrimages have been a sacred practice across cultures and religions for centuries. The act of embarking on a physical journey to a holy site or sacred place is believed to bring about spiritual growth, enlightenment, and connection to higher powers. For those on the path to spiritual enlightenment, pilgrimages can be a powerful tool for deepening one's spiritual practice and expanding one's consciousness.

When we set out on a pilgrimage, we leave behind the distractions and demands of our everyday lives and enter into a space of reflection, contemplation, and prayer. Whether we are visiting a sacred temple, a natural wonder, or a historical site, each step we take on our pilgrimage is a step closer to connecting with the divine within ourselves and in the world around us.

Pilgrimages offer us the opportunity to cleanse our minds, hearts, and spirits, and to release any negative energies or attachments that may be holding us back on our spiritual journey. By immersing ourselves in the sacred energy of a holy place, we can recharge and realign our chakras, allowing the flow of positive energy to awaken and activate our spiritual potential.

In the hustle and bustle of modern life, it can be easy to lose touch with our spiritual selves and the deeper meaning of our existence. By embarking on a pilgrimage, we can take a step back from our everyday concerns and reconnect with our innermost truths and beliefs. Whether we are seeking healing, guidance, or simply a deeper connection to the divine, a pilgrimage can offer us the space and time we need to commune with the sacred and awaken to our true purpose in life.

As we journey to sacred sites and connect with the energies of the earth and the cosmos, we open ourselves up to the possibility of receiving spiritual insights, wisdom, and blessings. By surrendering ourselves to the transformative power of pilgrimage, we can experience profound shifts in consciousness and personal growth that will ultimately lead us closer to spiritual enlightenment and inner peace.

**11**

# Chapter 11: Spirit Communication and Mediumship

# Connecting with the Spirit World

In the realm of spiritual enlightenment, connecting with the spirit world is a profound and transformative experience. For those who are drawn to the mysteries of the unseen realms, this practice can offer deep insights, healing, and guidance on their spiritual journey.

To connect with the spirit world, one must first cultivate a deep sense of mindfulness and presence. By quieting the mind through meditation and focusing on the breath, one can create a sacred space within themselves to invite in the energies of the spirit world. This practice requires patience, openness, and a willingness to surrender to the unknown.

Energy healing and chakra balancing can also play a crucial role in connecting with the spirit world. By working with the body's energy centers, one can clear blockages and open up channels for spiritual communication. This practice can help to align the physical, emotional, and spiritual bodies, creating a harmonious flow of energy that allows for a deeper connection with the spirit world.

Drawing upon ancient mysticism and esoteric traditions can provide valuable insights and tools for connecting with the spirit world. Shamanism and indigenous spiritual practices, in particular, offer powerful techniques for journeying into the unseen realms and communicating with spirit guides and ancestors.

Yoga and holistic wellness practices can also support one's connection with the spirit world. By cultivating a strong and flexible body, one can create a clear channel for spiritual energies to flow through. Incorporating breathwork, meditation, and mindfulness into one's daily routine can help to deepen one's connection with the spirit world.

For those interested in astrology and divination, exploring the cosmic energies can offer valuable insights into one's spiritual path. By studying the movements of the planets and stars, one can gain a deeper understanding of their own unique spiritual journey.

Crystal healing and gemstone therapy can also support one's connection with the spirit world. By working with the healing energies of crystals and gemstones, one can amplify their spiritual intentions and create a sacred space for spirit communication to occur.

Sacred geometry and metaphysical studies offer a deeper understanding of the universal patterns and energies that govern the spirit world. By exploring the intricate relationship between shapes, symbols, and energies, one can gain a greater appreciation for the interconnectedness of all things.

For those seeking a more immersive experience, spiritual retreats and pilgrimages can provide a powerful opportunity to connect with the spirit world in a supportive and nurturing environment. These sacred journeys can offer profound insights, healing, and transformation for those who are ready to embark on a deeper spiritual path.

Spirit communication and mediumship can be a powerful way to connect with the spirit world and receive messages from loved ones who have passed on. By developing one's intuitive abilities and opening up to the energies of the spirit world, one can become a clear channel for spiritual communication to flow.

In conclusion, connecting with the spirit world is a deeply personal and transformative practice that can offer profound insights, healing, and guidance on one's spiritual journey. By cultivating mindfulness, energy healing, ancient mysticism, and other spiritual practices, one can create a deep and meaningful connection with the unseen realms that will support and guide them on their path to spiritual enlightenment.

# Developing Mediumship Abilities for Spiritual Communication

Mediumship is the practice of communicating with spirits or entities from the spiritual realm. It is a powerful and profound way to connect with the higher energies around us and gain insights and wisdom from the other side. Developing mediumship abilities requires dedication, practice, and a deep connection to your spiritual self. To enhance your mediumship abilities, it is important to first cultivate a strong spiritual practice. This can involve daily meditation, mindfulness, and energy healing techniques such as chakra balancing. By grounding yourself and aligning your energy centers, you can create a clear channel for spiritual communication to flow through. Ancient mysticism and esoteric traditions have long held the belief in the power of mediumship for connecting with the spirit world. By studying these ancient practices and incorporating them into your own spiritual journey, you can deepen your connection to the spiritual realms and expand your mediumship abilities.

Shamanism and indigenous spiritual practices also offer valuable insights and techniques for developing mediumship abilities. By connecting with nature, working with sacred plants, and honoring the wisdom of indigenous cultures, you can tap into the ancient wisdom that has been passed down through generations. Yoga and holistic wellness practices can also support the development of mediumship abilities by balancing the mind, body, and spirit. By incorporating yoga postures, breathing exercises, and meditation into your daily routine, you can create a harmonious state of being that is conducive to spiritual communication.

Incorporating astrology, divination, crystal healing, and sacred geometry into your spiritual practice can also enhance your mediumship abilities. By working with these tools and modalities, you can deepen your understanding of the spiritual realms and expand your ability to communicate with spirits.

Ultimately, developing mediumship abilities for spiritual communication is a deeply personal and transformative journey. By exploring various spiritual practices and traditions, you can expand your awareness and open yourself up to the profound wisdom and guidance that the spirit world has to offer.

Milton Keynes UK
Ingram Content Group UK Ltd.
UKHW020632200324
439694UK00005B/14

9 781835 526439